Owoseni Adebowale, Germaine J. Imhanyehor

Service Oriented Business to Business e-Commerce: A Case Study of Cogwheel Incorporated

GRIN Publishing

Bibliographic information published by the German National Library:

The German National Library lists this publication in the National Bibliography;
detailed bibliographic data are available on the Internet at http://dnb.dnb.de .

Imprint:

Copyright © 2010 GRIN Verlag, Open Publishing GmbH
Print and binding: Books on Demand GmbH, Norderstedt Germany
ISBN: 978-3-640-82179-2

This book at GRIN:

http://www.grin.com/en/e-book/165457/service-oriented-business-to-business-e-
commerce-a-case-study-of-cogwheel

GRIN - Your knowledge has value

Since its foundation in 1998, GRIN has specialized in publishing academic texts by students, college teachers and other academics as e-book and printed book. The website www.grin.com is an ideal platform for presenting term papers, final papers, scientific essays, dissertations and specialist books.

Visit us on the internet:

http://www.grin.com/

http://www.facebook.com/grincom

http://www.twitter.com/grin_com

Blekinge Institute of Technology

Master in Informatics

Fundamental Issues in Informatics

Moment 4

Adebowale Oluropo Owoseni

&

Germaine Joy Imhanyehor

Discussion

System Integration

December 2010

Service Oriented Business to Business e-Commerce: A Case Study of Cogwheel Incorporated

Adebowale Owoseni & Germaine Joy Imhanyehor
Informatics Department, Blekinge Institute of Technology
Karlskrona, Sweden
{adow10, geim10}@student.bth.se

Abstract

The concept of eCommerce has evolved over the years from a conventional **"buy and sell"** *model where internet is merely a virtual market place; to a more robust, explicitly defined and seamless integration of businesses. The emerging eCommerce places emphasis on* **value creation**; *buyers have value for their money and are willing to pay for services, sellers equally derive values from income, information and knowledge available from processed data.*

This write-up, proposes a business to business (B2B) eCommerce system model to Cogwheel Incorporated; a manufacturing company that produces cogwheel. Cogwheel is a key component of car gearbox. The company intends to reduce administrative cost to almost zero through B2B. This paper considers the dynamics involved in implementing B2B with modern service oriented architecture.

1.0 Introduction

Imagine the world without internet. Sounds ridiculous! Sounds unimaginable! Can we then say that internet is the mother of all inventions? Yes. As arguable as it sounds, the advent of internet has redefined and still redefining many aspects of human endeavors, most obvious is what we call *information mobility* – the mechanisms surrounding the way information is being transported from one point to another and its interpretation in context and content. This information revolution has recorded great impact on business, it has changed the way and manner businesses operate irrespective of the industry. Now we can talk about e-commerce, e-business, e-service, XML, ontology, meta-language, ebXML, value chain and so on, these are emerging technologies that are shaping the online market place.

Business to Business (B2B) eCommerce framework describes the business transactions that take place between two or more companies, The consumers and supplies in these trades are always business entities rather individuals.[2] The fundamental challenge of this framework is how to move *'knowledge'* from one system to another; essentially, it borders on effective and efficient communication between independent and mutually exclusive systems. This communication could be achieved through *'services'* - a service is basically a re-useable component that is capable of changing business data from one form to another, it describes how data is accessed [6].

Similar to many software development principles, Service Oriented Architecture (SOA) abstracts the complexities involved in data manipulation (physical and logical mapping) by presenting to the user what he want and how it want it. According to Eri Thomas, service orientation provides a governing approach to automate business logic as distributed systems[3].

2.0 Problem description: Cogwheel and the business space

As shown in figure 2.0a; Cogwheel is an important component of a gear box, and the gear box is a car subsystem, it is a major component in car manufacturing.

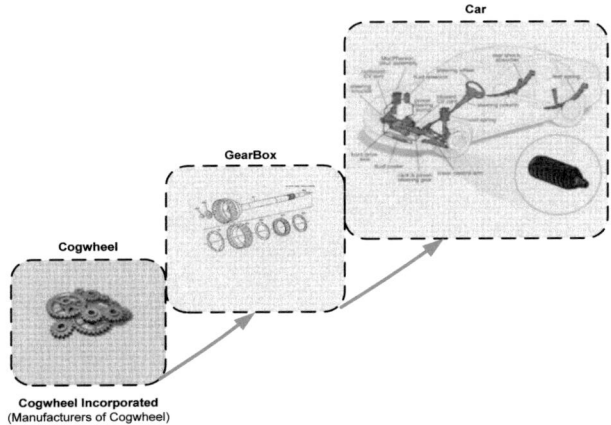

Figure 2.0a: Cogwheel in Car Context.

Cogwheel incorporated is a cogwheel manufacturing company; it directly transacts business with Gearbox manufacturing companies. It is good to note that different cars have different gear specifications; for example gear box for the Honda may not work for Hyundai, therefore Cogwheel incorporated's B2B platform should have the capacity to interface with as many brands of gearbox manufacturers as possible.

Figure 2.0b shows cogwheel business sphere as it relates with core business partners.

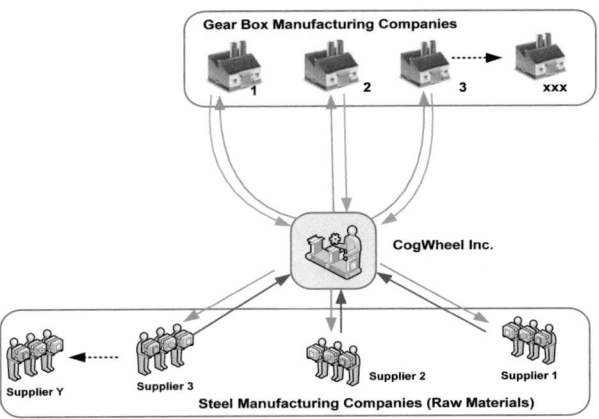

Figure 2.0b: Cogwheel business sphere.

What should cogwheel incorporated expect from the proposed B2B design? They are in four folds

1. Ability to exchange information with business partners *'when'* (right time) it is needed and *how* (right format) it is needed
2. Reduced turnaround time on business related transactions
3. Reduction in administrative cost
4. Access to pool of data that can produce knowledge when analyzed. This will in turn promote accurate business decisions. Information is a strategic asset [6] and it should be seen and treated as such.

3.0 Proposed B2B model

There are basically three types of businesses in the proposed B2B model (Figure 2.0b), no doubt these business entities have different processes, data structures and business rules that govern transactions. B2B will indirectly introduce a converging point to all the entities in the business network

Before we take a look at the B2B model, it will be good to find some answers to this question: What are the prerequisites for successful implementation of B2B?

- **Trust and Loyalty:** Transparency is not negotiable. As a matter of fact trust and loyalty is the foundational principle on which every other thing are built. Business entities must be *'open'* to each other. Data must be trusted and understandable [6]; integrating a B2B model is synonymous to incorporating an alien to your board of trustee or directors. *Only birds of the same feather could flock together successfully.* Slightest misrepresentation arising from distrust could ground the businesses in no time.

- **Standardization:** All business processes, requests and transactions should be standardized; there should be mutually acceptable and consistent methods of executing transactions. Semantics and syntax should be defined by the business entities within the network community. Although, the businesses are not expected to change their ways of doing things but the point of intersection with other business should be well defined and it should conform to agreed standards. It is this standard that will be used in building some form of intelligence into the system (*middleware*); coded in the meta-language (ontology).

- **Clarity:** All business units within the network must have a clear 'picture' of the essence of their partnership. Questions like - Why are we implementing B2B? Which part(s) of our business processes will be impacted by the partnerships? To what level are we going to encapsulate our transactions? What type of communication and technology are we adopting? How will this impact on cost and profitability? All these salient points raised by these question (and many more) should be well articulated and dimensions. Clarity is very essential

- **Independence:** Although one of the purposes of B2B is to find a converging point between member businesses, business unit should be able to operate as an independent entity. Utmost care should be taken so as not to trade freedom on the altar of synergy. The B2B solution should be system, platform or version independent [8]. The solution should be flexible enough to be able to accept new interface with new business entities.

- **Porter-wise:** It is strongly advisable that the business entities must operate within Michael portal's value chain theory – *"During the whole manufacturing process, nothing should be done except the customer is willing to pay for it in the end"* [7]. Since information processing consumes greater percentage of production time, business entities in the network should cooperate to reduce price to its possible minimum.

Now, let us take a look at our recommended service oriented B2B architecture as shown in figure 3.0a. The model primarily focuses on three factories, indirectly involved in the manufacturing of automobile (cars), our central point is on Cogwheel Incorporated because Cogwheel as a business entity is dual functional in the B2B model, it is acting as both consumer and supplier at the same time, a consumer of steel (for the production of cogwheel) and a supplier of cogwheel to the gearbox factory.

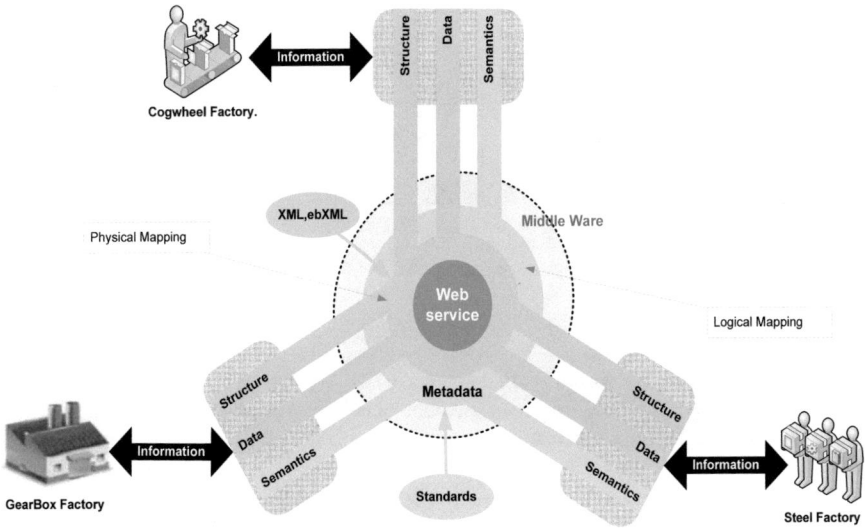

Figure 3.0a: Cogwheel B2B Architecture.

Three components are essential to this model

1. The **web service**, a medium for transporting information (to and from a given point) in a required format.

2. The **logical mapping** where standards are intelligently coded in meta-language so as to intelligently process metadata. This is ontology- deriving *meaning* from the *meaningless*

3. The **physical mapping** where structure and specified request could be mapped in XML and ebXML

All these components exist within a "*middleware*". Conventionally a peer to peer system is more secure but expensive to manage[8], it will be more challenging to incorporate new business entity into the B2B peer -to- peer network, we advice a partnership with a middleware central agency in order to reduce cost and promote greater flexibility. The issue of security is not very paramount once trust and loyalty is established within business partners. Of course, technical representatives of business entities within the network could form the middleware central agency.

Let us give a very simple information transfer scenario on our proposed B2B. Assuming Gearbox factory is placing an order for cogwheels to process 10 different types of gearboxes for different cars variant. All that will be specified in the order is the variant of cars and not the precise detailed specification of cogwheel required for each car variant. The middleware through embedded ontology will decipher the message and send understandable detail information to cogwheel as shown in figure 3.0b

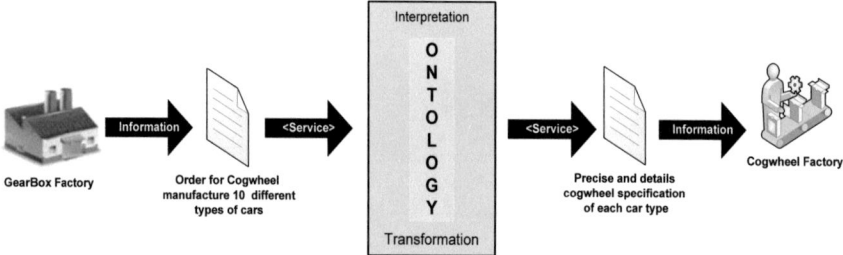

Figure 3.0b: Typical Information Processing

4.0 Conclusion

The model described in the section above promotes information retrieval at the right time and right format; it guarantees that information is available when it is needed. This will in turn reduce turnaround time as 95% of manufacturing process lies in information processing [6]. Definitely, cost will be reduced to barest minimum since information transfer is automated and faster, business entities will also have access to data that could be analyzed to make some intelligent business forecast and decision.

Central point of our service oriented B2B architecture is to effectively and efficiently transfer information from one point to another without altering its meaning (content and context). As simple as this may sound; players within the information network must very sensitive with the issues of trust, loyalty, standardization, clarity and independence. They should be *Portal-wise* by operating within the boundaries of value chain principle.

References

[1] Channabasavaiah, Holley and Tuggle, Migrating to a service-oriented architecture, *IBM DeveloperWorks*, 16 December 2003. Retrieve on the November 30th from http://www-128.ibm.com/developerworks/library/ws-migratesoa/

[2] EHow.com: Define Business-to-Business (B2B) Retrieve on the November 30th 2010, from http://www.ehow.com/about_4706934_define-businesstobusiness-bb.html#ixzz17VyEwl7M

[3] Erl Thomas, What is SOA? Design Paradigm. Retrieve on the December 5th 2010, from http://www.whatissoa.com/p4.php.

[4] Jonathan Timothy, Back to Basics – B2B. Retrieve on the November 30th 2010, from http://ezinearticles.com/?Back-to-Basics---B2B&id=4126783

[5] Mike Velle (2002). Service Oriented Architectures at General Motors (slides) SunnNetwork 2002 conference and pavilion retrieved on 5th Dec. 2010 from ebxml.org/presentations/sun_netwk_conf_10182002.ppt

[6] Paul A. Strassmann(2007). What is Service Oriented Architecture? (slides) retrieved on 5th Dec. 2010 from www.**strassmann**.com/pubs/gmu/**2007**-11-slides.ppt

[7] Per Flensburg. Integration of Information Systems - Moment 4 Guide. retrieved on 25th Nov 2010 from https://bth.itslearning.com/file/download.aspx?FileID=506233&FileVersionID=-1.

[8] Per Flensburg e-Services (slides) retrieved on 25th Nov 2010 from http://ikt.ei.hv.se/personal/impf/per/E-services-Steyr.ppt

[9] Per Flensburg. Ontologies (slides) retrieved on 25th Nov 2010 from http://ikt.ei.hv.se/personal/impf/per/OntologiesFensel.ppt

[10] Raghu R. Kodali (2005), What is service-oriented architecture? An introduction to SOA. Retrieve on the November 30th 2010, fromhttp://www.javaworld.com/javaworld/jw-06-2005/jw-0613-soa.html?page=1

[11] Wikipedia, Micheal Porter. Retrieve on the November 30th 2010, from http://en.wikipedia.org/wiki/Michael_Porter

[12] Wikipedia, Service Oriented Architecture. Retrieve on the November 30th 2010, from http://en.wikipedia.org/wiki/Service-oriented_architecture

[13] Wikipedia, Service Orientation. Retrieve on the November 30th 2010, from http://en.wikipedia.org/wiki/Service-orientation